SUCCESS
AGAINST ALL ODDS

REGINA O. OZOEMELA

SUCCESS
AGAINST ALL ODDS

FIVE SECRETS
OF RAPID CHANGE

ReadersMagnet, LLC

DEDICATION

Success Against All Odds is dedicated to my three children Faith, Love, and Peace, who themselves are now residing in the United States after having undergone some difficulties in life due to my ignorance. As they grow their families, it is my desire that they reach their highest potential and live fulfilling lives.

Acknowledgments

I'd like to say thank you to:

Jake, who supports and encourages me to be my best self;

John and his wife, my first role models, who were the financial and moral machine behind my success;

My father Adam, who left us a legacy of achieving our highest potential;

My mother Edith, who thought me how to love, give, forgive unconditionally;

My mentors and coaches who taught me how to overcome my fear of change, self-doubt, and limiting beliefs and establish my businesses with the mindset of multiple income streams. The following people whom I have been fortunate to receive mentorship and coaching from are: Loral Langemeier, Jack Canfield, Christian Mickelsen, Michelle Schubnel, Ali Brown, and so many others;

My writer and publishing team at Outskirts Press;

My host families, who let me into their homes on arrival from Nigeria, and provided me comfortable rooms to live and study in.

CONTENTS

INTRODUCTION

I AM AN AWARD-WINNING Professional Woman of the Year, recognized the National Association of Professional Women; I am a career and life coach who guides business owners, disadvantaged workers and women re-entering the workforce so that they can experience a successful and fulfilling life, both professionally and personally. Through my group and private individual coaching programs, I teach individuals to overcome limiting mindsets, take positive action, and achieve success defined on their terms. Most recently, I helped a carpenter make $20,000 in two weeks by tapping into his woodworking talents and helping him create an additional revenue stream. Now he's selling his own hand-crafted furniture in between residential renovation projects.

After struggling for several years as a poverty-stricken and divorced teen mother of three in Nigeria, I am passionate about helping men and women who feel stuck in their career and life to break through the perceptions, environment and mindset that hold them back from true happiness. A student of motivational speaker and *Chicken Soup for the Soul*® series author Jack Canfield,

I am an aspiring motivational speaker and author who has contributed a chapter to *Ready, Aim Captivate!*, a #1 Bestseller and International Bestseller at Amazon.com. I am also a contributing author of *Wounded, Survive Thrive!*, also an Amazon #1 International Bestseller and #1 Hottest New Release. I am a S.T.A.R.S award winner for my contribution to *Wounded, Survive Thrive!* I have also been awarded the Pinnacle Professional of the Year 2013 by Continental Who's Who in Recognition of Excellence.

In this book, I draw from my own frustrating experience of working 26 years in a low-level position at corporate job with little advancement, despite earning an MBA. I share with my clients the five steps I took to achieve the rapid change I needed to create my dream career. Personally, I overcame numerous roadblocks along my quest to finish high school despite being a teen mom, leave Nigeria to create a better life for myself and my young children, and obtain US citizenship. By transforming hardship into opportunity, persistence into achievement, I naturally inspire others to do the same.

I graduated from the University of Southern New Hampshire with a Master's in Business Administration. I volunteered for the American Diabetes Association and several educational programs, including Building Educated Leaders for Life, career day mentoring, and tutoring at local middle schools. I am currently a member of International Membership of Professional Advisors, Coaches, & Trainers (IMPAC), the United Methodist Church Health Ministry and Umuadaigbo (meaning the Igbo daughters) Massachusetts, an organization for women of a Nigerian tribe who live in Massachusetts.

I live in Boston, Massachusetts with my husband. I enjoy listening to music, dancing, singing, reading romantic novels, and watching political debates and campaigns.

The Power to Change our Lives
Lies Within Each of Us,
as Does the Power to
Realize Our Dreams

CHAPTER I

Growing Up in Nigeria

MY NAME IS REGINA Ozoemela. This book is about my life—my trials and tribulations, survival, and ultimate triumph over circumstances that seemed impossible to overcome. In writing this book, I want to reach out to those who are struggling in their lives. I want to inspire and empower others, to let them know what is possible if you remain focused, follow your dreams and intuition, and stay on high alert to recognize an opportunity when you see it.

In some ways, my story will seem very exotic to you…I was born in the remote village of Umosu Nsulu in Nigeria, and came to the United States as an exchange student. In other ways, though, it will be very familiar, and this is the point I most strongly want to make: no matter who you are, or where you are from, the principles of transcendence and success remain the same. Fear feels like fear, no matter where you are from. Pain and sorrow come to all people, regardless of nationality. Chances are that you won't have suffered in exactly the way I have suffered, but I think you will understand what happened in my mind and in my heart. Once you embrace the principle that suffering is suffering no matter who you are, then it is easier also to see that healing is healing, no matter who you are, and that the advice and actions that enabled me to succeed can empower you, as well.

The difference between those who make it in life and those who don't comes down to just one thing: the courage to strive for opportunities with dignity and self-confidence. There is no such thing as "easy success." Nothing worth having comes easily. Additionally, it's important to remember that our mistakes provide priceless learning opportunities. It makes no sense to cry over spilt milk. Don't let your obstacles discourage you—instead, allow yourself to find inspiration.

I am going to share my life story with you. Although the place I came from and the culture I grew up in may seem very different from yours, I think you will quickly see that the journey of the inner self from broken to whole is easily relatable to many different types of life experience.

I was born in a small village, where people lived off the land. They planted and harvested crops, living their lives by the clock and rhythm of the seasons. Community was important to us. The churches would schedule a Sunday ceremony during which each member of the congregation would present a portion of their crop for thanksgiving. These were times of celebration; families would invite relatives from other towns and villages to attend the Harvest Sunday service. There was entertainment, too—the choir would raise rich voices to showcase their songs; drummers would beat out a contagious rhythm; people would dance with joy when it was their turn to present their crops. The Monday following the Harvest Sunday service, a bazaar would be held, and church members would purchase the foodstuffs given to the church on Sunday, in order to raise money for church maintenance. Then the rest of the crops would be sold at the local market, and families would use that money to buy goods that they could not produce for themselves. When I think of life in the village, that is one of the things I miss…the gathering-together of people to share their abundance.

I grew up in the 1960s. Life in a small Nigerian village in the '60s was vastly different from the life I would later have in America. We had no running water, for example. We would go to the stream to fetch water, and carry it back. That doesn't sound like much of a chore, but imagine if you had to carry all the water you used, from a stream into your house. Water is heavy, and even simple tasks require a lot of it. Even though the weather was hot, when we wanted to take a bath, we would boil water and bathe in a zinc tub. Some families also boiled their drinking water, but most did not. Many people's houses were made of thatch. My father was one of the first people who built a zinc house. It had an asbestos ceiling.

We did not have electricity in the village. My father had a huge kerosene lamp that lit our whole compound, and all of our family who lived in the compound—my father's siblings and cousins, etc.—could all share the light. The light would stay on until midnight, to give everybody plenty of time to finish whatever they were doing. Frequently, in the silvery light of a glowing full moon, the children would gather in the compound with older people who would teach us folk songs and traditional dances. They would tell us stories, and we would exchange riddles and jokes until late into the evening. Our mothers would let us stay up for a long time, but finally they would shout for us to come to bed, because we had to be at school the next day.

The children often worked on handicrafts that were presented at school, and sometimes we would do community-based work at school—for example, we would have to go into the bush to get palm frond to repair our teacher's leaking kitchen roof. Other times, we worked on projects that we would use in our own lives. I remember sewing a dress by hand with needle and thread, and wearing the dress myself.

The community spirit that I mentioned earlier was also evident when it came to education. In northern and western Nigeria, the government provided everything for the students. But in eastern Nigeria, each family paid school fees or tuition for their children, and the villagers contributed money to build the school buildings. We used to take our own chairs and other equipment to school, until the village had accumulated enough money to provide those things for the students. I think part of the reason that the government treated us differently is that easterners are seen as very enterprising and self-directed. Maybe they figured we didn't need the same advantages as the rest of Nigeria.

Today, many of these aspects of village life have changed. There is now a bank, electricity, and many families have wells and running water. They use cell phones in the village today. None of these things were available when I was growing up; my memories are of a time and place very different from the modern world I know now.

The divorce of my parents was the most traumatic event of my childhood. I loved both of my parents very much. Family structure and culture around family are ways in which my life differed from the life of a typical American. My father was a very ambitious man who wanted to be educated. He had been trained as a tailor, and before we were born, he taught my mother the art of tailoring as well, so she made all our clothes. My father was well-known in his trade, and he decided to go overseas to continue studying his craft, in London. However, when he got to London, he realized that there were far greater opportunities for him in other fields. He studied industrial engineering, and when he came back to Nigeria, he worked for BP.

Although my father was a talented and ambitious man, and I appreciate the example he set for us to reach past limitations and consider how we could achieve more, my mother was victimized and abused in their marriage. She came from a wealthy family—which in our part of the world, meant that her family had many yam barns, sheep, goats, and fields—so while my father was away, my paternal grandfather was able to take good care of us financially. My mother was loving and intelligent, and a wonderful cook; even when she cooked for just the three of us, you would think she was catering a party. Her siblings and my father's relatives would often stop by to eat with us, because her food was so wonderful.

In my culture, it is usual for men to have more than one wife. My father had three wives. This complicated our lives because those wives, and their families, had an impact on me and my brother. For instance, my brother and I had to work very hard to ensure that the younger children of my father got some education, so that they wouldn't become perpetually dependent on us. Although they were not the children of our mother, family bonds and responsibilities are serious where I come from. Another way in which this affected my brother and me had to do with the way my stepmother, Alice, interfered with my parents' marriage in a malicious and destructive way.

My mother had a very hard time while my father was gone. She was responsible for the care of two little children—my brother and me—and in addition to that, she was victimized by a number of people in the village who decided to take my father to court in absentia, claiming that he had used their money to sponsor his overseas trip. This was not true; he worked in a coal mine to put himself through school. But in our culture, my mother was considered responsible in his absence. I remember several occasions sitting at the table eating dinner, when the police burst in, handcuffed my mother, and took her away from us. Between running her household and being harassed by the police, my mother was under a lot of stress.

Alice had originally come to our home as a maid, and my father married her. When my father went overseas, my stepmother became very wild in her behavior, sleeping with other men. She was jealous of my mother, and wanted to become my father's first wife. She wrote to my father and told him that my mother had boyfriends and was unfaithful to him. In our culture, when a couple divorces, the husband casts the wife out of the home; she is left to take care of herself, and he keeps the children. My father wrote to my mother and ordered her to leave. She refused; she was innocent. So, as soon as my father returned from

England, he arranged for the police to come and evict her from our home. They threw away all her belongings, and locked the door.

My brother John and I were left in the care of my father, stepmother, and paternal grandmother. I was a shy child, and felt very lost and alone. I missed my gentle, compassionate mother, and spent a lot of time by myself, crying, wondering why she had to leave. Much later, after my mother had remarried and had two children with her new husband, my father realized that his second wife had lied, and that he had been foolish to listen to her. He apologized to my mother, but of course, it was too late.

Many people experience the breakup of family through divorce. My situation may look a little different on the surface, due to the situation with my father's second wife, but the emotional impact was the same. I didn't understand what had happened, and it made me feel sad and insecure inside. When difficult things happen in children's lives, it's important for the people around them to provide support and care. I got that from my brother. He was nine at the time of my parents' divorce, and he was my role model. He loved me very much, and did not like to see me suffering. He helped me to come out of my shell of grief by using our mutual love of sports.

John would set up for track, long jump, and high jump in our compound. We had a big playground, and when we would get started, the other kids in the compound would join us. We would add hurdles and relay races when we had enough kids. Sports made both of us happy, and allowed us some distance from the pain of our mother's leaving. Sometimes we would even forget to do our homework, because we stayed up so late, playing into the night. We had other ways of sharing our closeness, too. My brother hated to do his chores, so I would help him out. He would give me some of the meat in his soup, and in exchange I would do the dishes for him. I remember many happy nights in our compound under the stars with him and the other kids, running ourselves into exhaustion, coming home with just enough energy left to take a bath and fall into bed. It was a great feeling.

I loved those days with my brother. But when John got older, he went away to boarding school, and I was left alone with my sorrow again. I had to find a way to manage it myself. In Africa, there are no such things as therapists or counselors. When things are hard, we had to figure out for ourselves what to do. I spent a lot of time depressed and crying before I realized that I could make the choice to fill my time differently. For me, creativity was the key to managing depression. I filled those troubled times with the things I loved to do. For example, I would pick up my hymn book and start singing my favorite songs. By the time I stopped, I would be filled with happiness.

Although I'm not a professional counselor, I strongly believe that anyone who is depressed or sad, and who doesn't have access to professional help, can find healing by following their deepest interests and engaging in a creative activity. By the time you finish, you will feel differently than you did when you started. When our minds are not in a creative mode, that's when the devil goes to work on us. I was too young to understand that the situation I found myself in wasn't my fault, and that I didn't have the power to change it. What I did have, though, was the power to live my life authentically despite those circumstances. We all have a deep need to connect to people. When you are vulnerable, it's important to make sure that you are connecting to people who will influence your life in a positive rather than a negative way. I will tell you about a choice I made that resulted in a negative connection, and what I did to get past it. I believe that if you've had a setback in life, by the time you finish reading this book, you'll know that it is possible to get yourself out of a bad situation and still live a purpose-filled life.

When my big brother left to go to college, I was still in high school. Where I lived, the student's family is responsible for school fees, unless you get a state or federal scholarship. You attend high school for five years, and at the end of that time, you take the West African School Certificate Examination. If you pass that exam, you are ready to enter college. In your fourth year of high school, you choose a concentration, which determines what your major will be in college.

My high school experience was different from most. I missed John terribly, and was still suffering from the breakup of my family. I was not comfortable at home, and I felt that I needed to escape. The method of escape I chose was not wise. I met a handsome man who was twenty years older than I, and I agreed to marry him despite my father's objections.

CHAPTER II

An Unwise Marriage

CHARLES (NOW MY EX-HUSBAND) was someone I had actually met long ago, though I didn't remember him at first. He came from a good family; his family and mine were family friends through our grandfathers. Both families were very close. Once when my father lived in Ibadan and the man who would become my husband lived in Lagos, my brother and I traveled to Ibadan to spend the long vacation with my father. He took us to Lagos for sightseeing, but we stayed so long that it was too late to travel home safely. Charles (whom at that point I had not yet met) went and stayed with a friend of his, giving his house to my father so he would have a safe place to stay with his family.

Several years later, I met him again when I was visiting the brother of a friend. I did not know who he was, and didn't make the connection—in fact, he himself never mentioned it until we had been married for several years. When we met at my friend's house, we struck up a conversation and introduced ourselves. We were irresistibly attracted to each other; he was tall and handsome, and I was a young girl without enough life experience to temper my attraction with a clear assessment of his character. I didn't even realize, at that time, how much older he was—he was an exceptionally attractive and youthful-looking man. Nothing happened at that time, but we kept in touch until he decided he was ready to marry, and came to me.

At first, I said no. I did not want to commit to marriage until I was finished with school. But he was very persistent. He even sent his mother to plead his case; she was in tears, saying that her son would not marry anyone else if I would not marry him. His family's house was a mile away from mine; he lived in the city and was a manager at SPAN (Screen Printers and Artists of Nigeria), a family business. He would come home every weekend, and it was convenient for him to visit me at my home, where we would spend time together. It was all very pleasant; my father was welcoming to him, and received him warmly.

That changed, though, when I told my father that Charles was interested in marrying me. My father said that he liked Charles, but he didn't want me to marry him. He refused to tell me why he felt this way. My heart was breaking, and I felt that my father hated me. He had driven my mother away from the house for no good reason, and now he would not let me marry the man I had chosen.

I tried to create mutual understanding between my father and me. I sat down with him one last time, to try to find out why he would not allow me to marry a man whom we knew to be from a good family, which is one of the most important criteria in choosing a spouse. My father said that he was refusing because I was too young, and did not know what I wanted. I felt a hot spark of rage inside me, at the implication that I was too stupid to know my own mind. My father also said that he wanted his daughters (me and my half-sisters) to complete our educations. That way, if things didn't work out in our marriages, we could take care of ourselves. When things started to fall apart between me and Charles, I was haunted by the sound of my father's voice, telling me that.

At the time, though, I was frustrated and confused. It wasn't as though there were anything wrong or unusual about the way Charles and I had met, or about our courtship. It wasn't as if we were unenlightened or illiterate, making an arranged match just with pictures or an introduction by proxy. I wasn't looking to marry a man who lived overseas, while I continued the life of a village girl. The only unusual facet of our relationship was the disparity in our ages.

However, I was not aware of just how wide that gap was. My father was right; I was too young to get married. It wasn't that I didn't know my own mind—I just didn't have enough life experience to fully understand all the red flags that were popping up in regard to Charles. For one thing, he never told me how old he was. I also didn't know that he was a high school dropout. I had grown up hearing stories from my grandmother about how men would choose a wife at a very young age—as young as six or seven—and nurture and train her to be his spouse. Then when she was a teenager, they would get married. So the idea of being a young bride didn't seem unusual to me.

My father's advice was good. Nobody should get married until they are at least twenty-five. But I wasn't in the mood to listen to my father. My heart was full of anger and resentment, and in order to teach him a lesson, I married against his better judgment. The real lesson turned out to be for me, though. Anger does not serve a delicious meal; instead, it gives you a reality that is hard to swallow.

My marriage to Charles did not turn out well. Although he promised that I could finish school after we were married, he did not honor that promise. He was a womanizer, and had no time to spend with me or with his children. Despite that, as I found out later from his brother, he was afraid of losing me if I completed my schooling. He had a vested interest in keeping me ignorant and therefore dependent. In addition to that, although I married him when I was in my sophomore year of high school, I had more education than he did, and he was intimidated by the idea of my having more schooling. He used the weapon that men have used for centuries to keep women under their control; he kept me pregnant, too busy bearing and raising his children to think of anything else.

Charles and I come from a polygamous culture, where it is perfectly acceptable for a man to have many wives, but not acceptable for a woman to have more than one husband. Women are taught that it is not their place to leave or seek divorce; they should just stay in their situation with the other wives, whether she likes it or not. I am glad to say that this has changed since the '60s and early '70s when I was enduring my marriage to Charles. Now, the women in that part of Nigeria are more educated and independent, and wouldn't put up with this kind of nonsense.

The main problem between Charles and me was that he neglected me and his children to pursue other women. One of the most distressing episodes in our marriage happened when Charles' sisters Jane and Linda held a meeting with me, accusing me of allowing their brother to have an affair with a married woman who was a family friend. They expected me to confront him about it. I hadn't heard about this, although it wasn't exactly a surprise; Charles was frequently unfaithful. Once, I had walked into our bedroom and caught him in bed with another woman whom I'd never seen before. There was no point to making a scene; I just walked back out and gave them a chance to get dressed and get out.

But even so, I never expected the call I got from his sisters, saying, "Why are you allowing our brother to have an affair with Mrs. Smith?"

I told them that Mrs. Smith was just a family friend, and I didn't think he was having an affair with her. They insisted that he was, but they wouldn't tell me how they knew. They were afraid that if it didn't stop, and Mr. Smith found out, that Charles' life would be in danger. Therefore, they wanted me to intervene before it went any further. I knew he would deny it even if it was the truth, but I asked him about it. His reaction was one of sorrow and anger. He was sad because he thought that his sisters were using me to stir up trouble in the family—and looking back on it, I now know that was exactly what was going on.

Jane said to Charles, "Why are you letting this girl upset you? I have told you to send her back to her father's home so I can get you another wife." Charles was disappointed and angry because this sister of his was old enough to be my mother, and he expected her to advise and protect me as she would her own daughter. But instead, she was plotting to split up our marriage. I did not fully understand this until I heard his reply: "Sister, what did this girl do to you, that you are plotting to destroy our marriage? Why don't you leave her alone? You may be able to harass me until I send her home, but still I won't remarry."

That was when it dawned on me that this sister might have been pulling many other tricks that I didn't know about, but she had revealed her hand in this one, and God was kind enough to put me in a position to overhear this conversation between them, so I would know that Jane was not trustworthy. I did not take any further action in this situation, because Charles realized that his sister had sent me to confront him, and that she was trying to stir up trouble between us, so that she could say, "I told you that your wife is a bad girl; now she is causing trouble in the family." I didn't want to play into her game, so I just let it drop. I didn't want my children to suffer if I got a reputation as a family troublemaker—in our culture, once a mother has made a bad name for herself, the family will take out their animosity on her children. I couldn't allow that to happen.

This episode is just one example of the drama and stress that went on in our marriage. While I was married to Charles, I couldn't go back to school, and I never held a job. I had to ask him for money, and was completely dependent on him. Sometimes we had huge arguments about money; other times he would be generous. I never knew what to expect. With three small children at home, I couldn't simply go back to school or get a job, unless he supported me in finding care for them. He refused to do this, because he didn't want anyone else raising his children. He told me that if I got a job outside the home, he would leave me. As it turned out, he effectively left me even though I complied with his demands, as he became involved with a woman old enough to be my mother, and gradually detached himself from his life with me and our children.

During my third pregnancy, I became restless and discontented. I needed to go somewhere for a change. I decided to visit my mother, who now lived with my stepfather in another city. Although I hadn't seen as much of her as I would have liked after my father divorced her, she and I had a close and loving relationship. I was happy that she had found my stepfather, who loved her dearly and cared for her with kindness. He was a good man who was also kind and accommodating to me and my brother John.

When I got there, my mother took me on social rounds, introducing me to some of her friends whom I hadn't met before. One of these friends was a prophetess. This woman said to me, "I have nothing to offer you, but I'll pray for you." She instructed my mother and me to kneel down, and we did. After she finished praying, she told us what had been revealed to her about Charles. She said that my husband had "moved away" from me, and that she couldn't tell whether or not he would return. She also said that I shouldn't try to do anything about it; I should just pray, and allow the will of God to manifest.

This disturbed me. I remembered how hard things had been for me and my brother after my parents' divorce. I didn't want my children to suffer in the same way, and I had always told Charles that no matter what happened, I would never leave my children. The prophetess did not give me any details about what "moving away" meant…I didn't even know whether she meant emotionally, or literally, or both. She gave me some Bible passages to read for strength and comfort.

Little did I know that he was actually leaving his family for an older woman in the military. I had no clue; at this time, everything was peaceful between us—no quarrels, no animosity. However, when I returned home, I kept the words of the prophetess in mind, and started paying more attention to his habits. I noticed that he was working late a lot. Then he started traveling two or three days at a time; or sometimes, he would stay away just overnight and come home the next morning. Then, he started going to parties with a "military friend," but I was never invited. I assumed that this friend was a man.

"Does your military friend know that you have a wife and children?" I asked.

"Yes," he admitted.

"Then you should invite your military friend—who seems to have no name—over for dinner, so we can get to know him and he can meet your family," I suggested.

He never responded to that idea. I knew something was seriously wrong, but I didn't know exactly what it was. Charles' older brother was always fighting with him now, but I didn't know why. It was because he had told Charles to stop his affair with this woman, and things had turned ugly between them. Charles' entire family knew about this situation with the other woman, but nobody was telling me. Polygamy was accepted in our culture, but even so, this affair was kept secret.

My sister-in-law Jane called a meeting with me and Charles' brother's wife. She said to us, "Your husbands are both trying to get married again, but I don't know which of them will marry first."

We looked at her and at each other, dumbfounded. I was both surprised and not surprised, because the prophetess had told me that Charles was moving away from me, and I had noticed the strange changes in his behavior.

I am of apostolic faith, so I believe in prophecies. One day while I was still pregnant, Jane and I took a walk. There was an apostolic church along the way. I had told Jane that I was feeling dizzy, so when we got to the church, she suggested that we go in and pray, although neither of us was a member of the church, and we knew nobody there. The pastor of the church was praying for someone when we tiptoed in and sat down. After he finished his prayer, he asked if he could help us. Jane said yes, and told him that I was feeling dizzy.

"That sometimes happens to pregnant women," he said with a compassionate glance at my swelling belly. "You should go home and lie down. Make sure that you are getting enough rest."

He asked us to kneel, and we did. He prayed for both of us. When he finished praying, he said to me that my husband's life would be in danger if he didn't turn away from the path he was headed down. He said to me, "You have no control over what is happening. It is not your fault; it is meant to happen that way because that is the way God wants to lift you up, so don't do anything about it." He asked me to read Psalm 35.

When we left the church, Jane said, "Don't pay attention to him. Don't read that Bible passage he gave to you—who would you be reading that passage against? Would it be against me, or your husband?"

Deep down inside myself, I knew that Jane must be involved in the collapse of my marriage, since she resented my reading the Bible for my own support and comfort. As if she hadn't done enough damage, she then took me to the army barracks, to the office of the woman my husband was about to marry (though I didn't know this at the time) and asked her to give me a shot. Luckily, this woman was a trained nurse who knew that it wasn't safe to give just anything to a pregnant woman, so she refused.

I still ask myself why I didn't stay away from Jane. I often had a bad feeling about her, and she caused me a lot of pain. At the same time, I hungered for a mother figure. I had never gotten over my mother leaving our family when I was so young. I had been deprived of her care and love in some strange ways—for example, she would make clothes for me, but my paternal grandmother, who was taking care of me, would not allow me to accept or wear them. Sometimes, my brother John was able to make arrangements for gifts from my mother to be transmitted to me through one of my aunts. But still, this was emotionally confusing. I was always in search of a reliable mother, because I had not yet learned to mother myself. Jane wasn't a good choice, but we do the best we can with the knowledge we have.

When Charles got ready to marry his mistress, he played a cruel trick on me in order to get me out of the way. My relationship with my father had been painful for many years. He hadn't ever accepted my decision to marry Charles, and we hadn't spoken to each other for a long time. Charles told me that my father had contacted him and requested that he bring me and the children home for a visit. I was overjoyed to hear that, after all this time, my father had finally forgiven me and wanted to spend time with me and his grandchildren. I happily agreed, Charles took me back to the family compound, and…he left me there.

After nine months, Charles stopped coming to visit us. I started to hear rumors that he had gotten married. Even my father heard this rumor, and sent a delegate to attend the wedding, to be sure that it was not just gossip. As it turned out, it was the truth. My father didn't understand why Charles was neglecting me. He asked why Charles had stopped coming to visit, and asked if I had quarreled with him or done something to alienate him. I said that I hadn't. My father sent for Charles and asked him when he would be coming to take his family back. Charles told my father that he and his new wife were building a mansion in the city which would include a wing for our children, and that Charles would send his father to fetch us, and we would live with his family while the house was being built. Although this didn't sound particularly appealing, there was not much my father could say about it, since he was a polygamist himself.

My father-in-law came to get me as promised, but he came without his wife. This was a clear signal that my mother-in-law did not want me back in the family. We had already heard from a family friend that her attitude toward me was not welcoming; her feeling was that her son had sent me back to my father, and that if he brought me back into the family, it would be at his own risk. My mother would have understood the significance of this right away, and would never have let me go with my father-in-law. But my father, who always considered his own convenience over the well-being of those who were dependent on him, let me go.

Although the cultural norms I grew up with were different from what many of my readers have experienced, I know that there are many people who have suffered the heartbreak of an irresponsible spouse, and who have been at the mercy of family members who did not have their best interests at heart. This type of vulnerability and pain translates across continents and lifestyles. The pain of being betrayed and disappointed; the desperation of being dependent on someone who is unreliable—these sufferings are as old as time. And so I know that the actions I started to take in order to save myself contain valuable lessons for everyone.

When you are vulnerable, when you are dependent, the strongest thing you can do for yourself is to try to plan an exit strategy. I know that it may seem impossible; that your circumstances feel overwhelming. Mine did, too. I was still a teenager, with three small children. I had not finished high school. I was living in a patriarchal culture that didn't encourage women. I had a husband who behaved shockingly toward me. I was living with people who disapproved of me. This was a lot to deal with. But I chose to look for and nurture the ray of light inside me that kept saying: "You can do better. You can be better."

When things are really difficult, it makes sense that you'll be overwhelmed by figuring out a plan. You have to start with one step at a time. You may not be able to formulate an overall strategy, but if you start to look, you will be able to identify a positive action you can take. It may be as simple as choosing to recognize the beauty of the sky when you look out the window in the morning. It may be as personal as committing to prayer or meditation. But there is always something you can do, and each simple positive action leads to another.

In my case, I wanted to figure out how to go back to school. I had married Charles with his promise that I would be able to finish school, and he had never fulfilled that promise. I had no money for school, Charles wouldn't help me, my brother John was still at the university, and my father had retired. The positive action I took was to play along with the plan set out for me, until I could figure out how to get back to school. But I was not committed to living a life run by other people. I was biding my time, looking around for an opportunity.

Chapter III

Learning to Break Free

THE GREATEST CHALLENGE IN changing my circumstances lay in the fact that I had a three-month-old baby. I could not imagine leaving her. What I didn't know at the time was that John was also crafting a strategy to get me back to school, and he was taking into consideration that the baby would need to be older before this was possible. He suggested that I start reading newspapers and magazines to get my knowledge base current, so that I would be ready to go back. And he contacted our aunt, who agreed to allow me to live with her while I was in school. This plan was devised and settled by my aunt and my brother. My aunt agreed to take care of my tuition, food, and clothing with the understanding that my brother would reimburse her once he finished his own education and got a job.

I was very fortunate to have a brother who cared about me so much, and an aunt who was willing to support his plan to help me. I know that not everyone has that type of support. However, I think it is true that for many people, opportunities and support are available. They may require a change of heart or personal sacrifice to accept. My struggle was to decide what would cause the least damage to myself and my children in the long run. I paid a stiff price for my poor decision when I married Charles, and that price continued to be paid by my family and my children. I could have further made the decision to stay captive to that marriage, and to live and die under the thumb of my husband's family. In many ways, that would have been the easier decision. I knew, though, that although breaking free would cause stress and damage to me and to my children, it would be better than setting an example of passivity and inaction. When life presents you with great challenges, sometimes you have to weigh the lesser of two evils, and make choices that will disrupt your life but will be better in the long run.

The life that Charles had set up for me was not acceptable for me or for his children. He still visited very seldom, and when he did visit, it would be very early in the morning when the children were asleep; he'd would go and see his mother, and then leave. One afternoon he showed up. I had been working on the farm and had come back to take a bath. Our oldest daughter, who was five years old at the time, ran to tell me that her father was around. By the time I had come back out to tell him that we needed money for food, he had left without asking to see me or the children. I was told that he had gone to the city eight miles away from where we were, and that he would come back before heading back to the city where he lived. He did return, but once again, he did not stop to see the children and me. He went straight to his mother's house, jumped in the car, and left. I started sending messages that we were out of food, and that we needed money. The children needed clothing. We were out of everything.

"My son is married now. She should go home," Charles' mother said. But I couldn't go home; my father had given me to Charles, and Charles had put me here with his family. "If she doesn't go," my mother-in-law said, "I will treat her in such a way that she will be forced to leave."

She put a lock on her bedroom door and locked up all the food. She would then pick up her Bible and go out to spread the Good News. She wouldn't come back until afternoon, and that whole time, we would go hungry. I was still breastfeeding my youngest child; I needed nourishment to feed him properly, and my older children were hungry. Sometimes I would take the children to friends' houses, and they would feed us while my mother-in-law was gone. I knew that I had to take drastic measures when one day Charles sent his younger brother to bring us some supplies. He sent a loaf of bread, two cans of milk, a tin of Ovaltine, and a pack of sugar. My mother-in-law took the supplies, showed them to me, divided them up, gave me the smaller portion for myself and my children, and told me to let her know when we were finished. There wasn't enough there to make a decent meal for one person, let alone a breastfeeding mother and two children. I realized that she wanted me to die of hunger.

Alone, on foot, I escaped from her house with my children. I did not tell her or my father-in-law that I was leaving. I walked the mile to my hometown, my baby in my arms, my children following me. I told my father that I was done with the marriage. He advised me to go to the city and confront my ex, to tell him that I'd had enough, and to give him the option of either letting all of us stay in the city with him, or leaving the children in his care so I could return home. These both seemed terrifying to me. What if he wanted me to stay with him? I would never be able to go back to school; I would be under his thumb for the rest of my life. But even worse…what if he told me to go, and kept my children? With no education and no job, I couldn't afford to keep them without his support. If he said he wanted them but didn't want me, I wouldn't have a choice. We were literally starving. I had lost so much weight that my ribs were visible through my skin.

I cried all the way from my father's home to Charles' office in the city. When he saw me he jumped up right away; he took the baby from me and hugged our two older children.

"Why have you come to the city?" he asked. "Do my parents know you're here?"

I told him that his parents did not know I had left, but that I was at the end of my rope; they treated me and his daughters like outcasts, and were slowly starving us. I told him I was desperate. I had no job and no money; everything he sent to his parents' house for me was confiscated by his mother; my own mother had her own family now, and I couldn't ask her and my stepfather to take us in when my husband, the father of my children, was alive and well and perfectly capable of taking responsibility for us.

Charles stopped what he was doing and told us to get in the car with him. It seemed to me that he had a plan of some kind. I was so tired of trying to figure out what to do next; it was a relief to let him take charge, even for a little while. He drove me to his oldest sister, Grace, and told her to talk to me about why I had come to see him. He went to get food for me. He came back with a bag of rice, a bag of beans, five dozen eggs, a bag of African yams, and lots and lots of vegetables. At this point, I had made up my mind that there was no going back.

I told Grace how her mother was treating me and the children. She knew her mother well enough not to be surprised by what I was saying, but she was extremely apologetic, and wanted to know if there was anything she could do to make up for it. I told her that the children and I simply couldn't go back to live with her parents, and that the only thing anyone could do to make me happy would be to send me back to school.

"I'm happy for Charles; I truly am," I told her. "He's married now to a woman with money, who has promised him that she will buy him a brand-new car, that she'll build a mansion for him in his father's compound, and send his children to military school."

"But when he married her, he didn't realize that she would do all those things only if you were out of the way," Grace said.

I nodded. I knew what had happened…or at least, what he claimed. His original plan was not to let me go, but to get everything he could from her, and then divorce her. I had asked him once, before things got out of hand, why he was marrying her. "She has too much money and is looking for a man to have a joint account with, so the government will not question why she has so much money, since she is only a civil servant," he told me. She was about twenty years older than he was, a military nurse who had attained the position of captain. Before she retired, she was promoted to major. Somehow, she was in a position to steal government money, and she had stolen so much of it that she needed a joint account to hide it. That was what this woman told my ex, and he bought into it, not realizing the price he would pay to acquire her wealth. He would have to lose me to do it; she wanted me gone. That was why he visited so seldom, and seemed to take so little interest in me and his children. He had put himself in a very bad position, and did not know what to tell me.

Grace listened to everything I had to say. She was about the same age as my mother, and I hoped she would have some good advice for me. She suggested that Charles should find an apartment for me and the children to live in, where he could visit me and make babies, and we would be out of the way of his second wife.

"No," I said. "My mind is made up. I need to go back to school, so that I will have an education and the option to support myself. All I need to know is that my children will be cared for."

Again, gently, she suggested the option of my living in an apartment.

"Grace, listen. You have a daughter my age. If she were married, and in a situation like mine, would that make you happy?"

She admitted that it wouldn't.

"Wouldn't you want to see her do anything she had to do, to get her life back, to take care of herself, and to give herself a chance in life?"

She nodded. And she gave me one of the gifts that allowed me to go back to school. She agreed to take my children and care for them. She was a teacher and her husband was the headmaster of a school. They also had a farm, so they were comfortable and prosperous. I felt that of all the people I knew, I would be able to trust her to care for my children. I also knew, even then, that my decision would come at a price. Later in life, I would have to work very hard to rebuild my relationship with my children. But there wasn't a better way out for me, and so I left my children with Grace. I visited them to wash their clothes and play with them, but it wasn't the same as having me there all the time. As I walked away, I remembered my own pain and confusion when my mother had to leave. I understood a little better now how she must have felt.

Chapter IV

An Unexpected Opportunity

I DID NOT KNOW how I would get the money to go back to school. My father had retired from BP, and had dumped his severance pay into starting a convenience store, which wasn't doing as well as he had hoped, so he had no money to help me. My brother was in his final year at the university, and after that he had to serve a year in the national youth corps before he could look for a job, so it would be a while before he started making money. I knew, though, that I had to focus on the goal, not on the obstacles. This is another of the lessons I learned that applies to many situations. If you focus on why you can't do something, you'll never do it. If you focus on what you want to do, unexpected opportunities may present themselves.

I went to work for my father at his convenience store. I did the best I could, and prayed that something would happen to allow me to go back to school. One day while I was at the store, the mailman came. I took the mail from him before it was all delivered to my father, and to my surprise, there was something for me. It was a letter from my brother, telling me to ask our father for money to travel to my aunt's house. Admission to the high school in the city where she lived had been secured for me. I was so happy that I literally jumped for joy, then fell and sustained some hard bruises.

In this letter, John was angry with me for ignoring his first letter, which meant that I should already have been in school by the time I got the second letter. I realized that my father must have opened the first letter—usually he sorted the mail, and I didn't handle it at all. I made a lot of sales at the store, and he didn't want to lose the money I was making for him. This was very selfish on his part, but I didn't want to confront him about it; I was happy to simply move on. All I wanted was to get the travel money from him, and move on with my life. Everything was now out in the open, and he would have to answer to my brother for the first letter that he had stolen from me.

The confrontation between my father and John was an emotional one. John seized the opportunity to remind my father of the hardship he had put us through by divorcing our mother, and how as a result of my confusion and pain, I tried to escape through this ill-advised marriage to Charles, which caused me even more suffering. For the first time in his adult life, my father was seen to cry like a baby. His tears could not heal the wounds of the past, but at least he did the right thing and gave me the money to travel to my aunt's house.

I went back to school as a sophomore, which was where I had stopped before I got married. I was doing well in school, sure that my children were in good hands.

I participated in sports, and enjoyed the academics. In my junior year, I had an incident with a geography teacher who wanted to take advantage of me. He wanted to date me, but I refused. I had saved all of my papers during the school year, because I was proud of my good grades. My grade on the final exam was good, too. But when my report card came, I had almost a failing grade in the class. My aunt was angry with me. I told her that something was wrong, and pulled out all my papers to show her that I had done well in that class all year. We took all the papers and my report card to the school principal, and she agreed that something wasn't right. She sent for the teacher to come and explain himself, but he ran away, and that was the last we saw of him until the principal was transferred to another school. However, my report card was corrected to reflect my good grades. I learned a valuable lesson about the importance of correct documentation and paperwork, and I was glad that I had saved my papers during the year.

I would walk five miles to school and five miles home every day. Sometimes my aunt would give me money to take a cab, but I always saved it to send to my father to keep for my children, so that if they needed anything, they could go to my father and get the money. I was very glad that my relationship with my father had improved to the point that I was able to trust him with this. After the incident with the geography teacher, my aunt realized that I could do better by living at the school boarding house. Although this was more expensive, she saw how well I had done in my sophomore year, and felt that I deserved the chance to do even better. She was right; my grades got even better once I no longer had to walk ten miles a day. I still walked to my apostolic church five miles away every Sunday, but at least that was just once a week, and not every day.

One Sunday I waited for the prophetess, a member of the church whose job it was to pray for people who come to ask for prayers when the church is not in session. She lived near the premises so that church members could call on her at any time of the day or night. She would pray for people both individually and in groups. I wanted to ask her to pray for me because my exams were approaching. As she was praying for me, she said that she saw me flying. I shrugged and did not take this seriously, because I have no literal wings, and certainly I had no plans to take a trip by airplane. She insisted, though, that I would be flying somewhere far away from Africa.

Later that month, my brother married his high school sweetheart, and I was one of the bridesmaids. I was proud of my brother and how he was living his life—he and his fiancée waited until they graduated from university before getting married. He used his microbiology and chemistry majors to get a good job with a pharmaceutical company, The Welcome Foundation. His wife also studied medicine, and landed a job as an ophthalmologist with the federal government. I was so happy to see them married, and honored to be a bridesmaid. I liked one of the photos that the wedding photographer had taken of me, and I stopped by the studio to get a copy. Little did I know that visiting the photography studio that day would change my life.

One of the photographer's friends was the director of an exchange program called "Experiment in International Living." When I went to get my photo, I overheard them discussing the exam that he was going to administer to his students who were planning to travel to the US as exchange students. It had never entered my mind to study in the US, but as I heard him talk, I felt very strongly that I should ask him about it. This is one of the important lessons of success: when something catches your attention strongly, even if it is something completely unexpected or out of the realm of your experience, act on that sense of urgency. Opportunites don't always come along looking like we think they will. Success in life depends upon being willing to follow a path that may open up where there seemed to be no way out… even if that path leads to a destination you might not have dreamed of.

I approached the program director and asked him for information about how the program worked. I found out that he still needed to fill one space! I applied for the opening, and was invited to take the test. When the test results were returned from the US…I had been selected! I would finish my twelfth year of schooling in the US, and would receive my high school diploma there. I would live with an American host family, and we would learn about each other's cultures as well.

Chapter V

Going to America

ALTHOUGH I HAD BEEN given this extraordinary opportunity, as usual, my father wasn't particularly supportive, even though this adventure could change my life, and he himself had gone abroad to study and had benefited greatly from the experience. He said he was worried about all the gang violence in the States, and he thought the weather would be too cold for me to endure. So he refused to sign any of my documents. My aunt and my brother stepped in to act as my sponsors. They signed all my paperwork, and assumed financial responsibility for my stay in the US. I tried to take my family's concerns seriously. I signed up to stay with a Christian host family, feeling that I would be safer there. My aunt, who had studied in the UK, told me that things would be difficult because it would be hard for me to understand spoken American English, and that the Americans would find it hard to understand me, too. She also warned me about how cold I would feel, and how different the food would be. I wasn't unrealistic; I knew there would be challenges, and I knew that the one-week orientation provided by the program couldn't be adequate to prepare us for life in a completely different culture.

I was ready for all of it, though. I knew that one of my greatest strengths was in my adaptability. I'd had to learn how to make the best of difficult circumstances from an early age, and I was good at it. I arrived at JFK Airport in New York in August, and was picked up in a bus along with four other students to travel by road to Brattleboro, Vermont for orientation. My family had been right—summer weather in the US felt cold to me, after the 110-degree temperatures I'd come from. I didn't even want to go outside to interact with the other students…I was just too cold!

After the orientation, I traveled to my final destination of Manchester, New Hampshire to live with my Christian host family, who were Baptists. They had originally come from the Netherlands, but they were US citizens. It was interesting living with Americans who were originally from another country. My host father was Reverend Keith, and he was the minister of his church. His wife, Maria, was a homemaker; sometimes she went to volunteer at group homes, helping people who couldn't take care of themselves. They had three children: Richard, Anita, and Yvonne. They were caring and loving people who treated me as if I were their own child. Since they themselves had adjusted from a different culture, they were especially compassionate toward my need for time to settle in and get used to things. I had the luxury of a room all to myself in their four-bedroom home.

I liked living with them, but there was one aspect of life with this host family that puzzled me—the children and I ate only one hot meal a day, and that was our school lunch. For dinner we often had peanut butter and jelly sandwiches. On the weekend, we had one hot meal on Saturday, and one on Sunday. Then I noticed that Anna and Keith would cook a hot meal after the children went to bed. I was puzzled by this, especially having come from a family where my mother's bounty and hospitality with food was part of the values I absorbed while growing up. I got curious enough to ask, and Anna and Keith told me that they couldn't afford to feed everyone a full hot meal three times a day. We got our hot meal at school, and they allowed themselves one hot meal at home, but they couldn't bear the thought of cooking a meal and not sharing it with the children, even though they couldn't afford to, so they waited until we were in bed before they cooked and ate their one substantial meal of the day. I felt for them—I remembered only too well what it was like to have trouble making ends meet—and had not realized until I asked this question how tight money was for them. They never made me feel as if I were imposing on them in any way. I sometimes offered to help purchase groceries for the family, but they wouldn't accept that. Eventually, Anna and Keith and my three foster siblings were transferred out of state, and I went to live with an Irish family, the Connors.

Mrs. Connors was older than Anna; she was retired, and her husband had passed away a long time ago. She still had four children living at home when I was staying with her; one of them went back and forth between home and a girlfriend's house. The youngest child in the family, Laura, was about my age and we went to church together; it was she who had asked her mother to take me in after my first host family left the state. I got along well with the family—for a while, Laura's older brothers made fun of my accent, but I learned to tease them back, and that stopped them! As with my first host family, I had my own room. Mrs. Connors was a great cook, and there was plenty of food. She was very supportive of me and my studies, and sometimes she even bought me gifts, which was very generous of her. Toward the end of my exchange program, I socialized with some other Nigerians who found me and had a party for me after they read about me in the *Manchester Union Leader*, which published an article about how I had made the honor roll at Central High School. Knowing them helped me to transition out of high school to Southern New Hampshire University, where some of them were students.

Although I hadn't been in the US for very long, I'd learned a lot during my studies at the American high school. When I first arrived, I had a lot of anxiety because it was hard for me to understand what the teachers were saying. I had been warned that this would happen, but I didn't know how long it would last. For three solid months, I could not understand the teachers, and they couldn't understand me, either, because of my accent. I compensated for this gap by diligently studying my textbooks; often, I was ahead of the rest of the class. Sometimes when I knew the answer to a question, I didn't raise my hand, because the other students would laugh at the way I spoke. But the teachers were aware of the situation, and knew that if they requested a written answer from me, I would get it right. My strength was more in written English, due to my accent. I thought at first that I would never get used to being laughed at, but with the passage of time, it stopped…either because the kids got tired of laughing, or because I got used to it, and so we all just got along.

I always stayed focused on my mission, which was to get an education and work toward a better life. I was aware of the sacrifices my brother and aunt had made to help me, and I was determined to be worthy of their support, and to become the person I knew I could be. I had to shrug off not only teasing about my accent, but also I had to ignore ignorant opinions about Nigerians in general. There was a prevailing stereotype that Nigerians are criminals—but of course, there are criminals everywhere in the world. I had been told that America was dangerous and full of gangs, but I didn't let that influence how I perceived the people around me. There are good, hard-working Nigerians in all walks of life: employees, business owners, and law-abiding citizens who make a living in the US, with no criminal record at all. There are also some who bring a bad name to their country, and who can't seem to stay out of prison. I know I'm not one of those, so people can say what they like, and it doesn't concern me. If I stay focused on my goals, I will succeed, and success is where I choose to put my energy.

After I graduated from high school, a new dilemma faced me. I was in the US on an educational visa, and if I didn't stay in school, I couldn't stay in the States. Even if that hadn't been the case, though, I wanted to continue my education so that I could get a good job. I wanted to attend the University of New Hampshire, Durham to study nutrition and dietetics, but they didn't want to deal with the complexities of my visa status. So, although it wasn't ideal for me, I secured admission to Southern New Hampshire University, a business school, where I majored in general management. Although it wasn't the school I wanted to attend, I was very grateful to their foreign students advisor, who explained that I couldn't change the type of visa I had, but as long as I stayed in school in good financial standing, I would be legal. He got me another four years of legal status, on the condition that I remained in school and my tuition was paid. My brother generously paid my tuition from start to finish, which he could afford to do because he had a good job, and he and his wife had not yet started their own family.

After I graduated from high school, I moved out of the Connors' house and into an apartment in town, where it would be easier to catch the bus to school. Two months after I moved, there was a fire, and I lost everything, including my books. The university was generous enough to donate replacement textbooks, other students donated clothes, and my church donated household items so I had the basics I needed to continue my schooling. I stayed with my Nigerian friends until I found an efficiency apartment, where I stayed until I graduated. Through all of this, I stayed focused, with the idea that I could get a better job and make a better living. However, I was naïve about how precarious my visa situation was. I would eventually come to understand that if I wanted to continue to live in the US, I had to perpetually remain in school. Otherwise, I would have to go home and serve my country for two years before applying for another visa to return.

Chapter VI

Working My Way Up from the Bottom

I HAD TO FIGHT with everything I had not to go back to Nigeria. In other countries, it would be possible to go home and come back, but Nigeria is so incredibly corrupt that I wouldn't be able to get another visa without bribing the officials, and my brother, who would have to give me the money, didn't believe in giving or accepting bribes, a stance I respected and agreed with. Therefore, I did everything I could to stay in America. After I got my bachelor's degree, my brother told me that I should go on to get a master's degree. He wanted me to be as well-qualified as possible, but also, he wanted me to be able to stay in the US, which I couldn't do unless I was still a student. There were no jobs at home, even if I had wanted to return to Nigeria.

School wasn't the only thing on my mind, though. I still had three children at home whom I had to support. Per the terms of my agreement with the school, I wasn't supposed to work off-campus, but I had no choice—the work-study jobs available at the school didn't pay enough for me to support myself and still send money home for my children.

Not too long ago, I read a story on CNN.com titled "From scrubbing floors to Ivy League—homeless student to go to dream college." I read through the whole article, and learned that this student had been abandoned by her drug-addicted parents. Someone helped her to find a job as a janitor at a school where she became a straight-A student, and eventually she was admitted to Harvard University, all expenses paid. She remained focused on what she wanted out of life and how to get it, as long as she was able to keep a roof over her head. I admired this girl and appreciated her story; it reminded me of the things I had to go through when I was trying to balance my dream of getting an education with the necessity to work. I remember those days very well, and because of my experiences, I am always kind and respectful to everyone, no matter what kind of job they are doing. I had some pretty menial jobs myself, out of necessity.

For a while I worked in the housekeeping department of the Sheraton Hotel, cleaning rooms and making beds. My coworkers always talked about how much money they made in tips, which puzzled me, because I was making only my hourly wage. Little did I know that when my supervisor made her rounds, she picked up the tips out of the rooms. One week when she was on vacation, I made $250 in tips. The moment she came back, she took all the tips again. I couldn't say anything about it; I was afraid she would report me to the school, since I wasn't supposed to work off campus. I was supposed to wear a uniform at the Sheraton, which I found demeaning. When the supervisor called me in to enforce the uniform policy, I decided to quit. The tips are the benefit that makes that kind of job worth having, so I realized that there wasn't anything worthwhile keeping me there.

I worked a variety of lower-level jobs, including at a shoe factory and a sweater factory, at Montgomery Ward as a sales associate, and as an office cleaner. I often worked night shifts during my undergraduate studies so I could come home and then go to school. Some of my jobs were from 3 p.m. to 11 p.m., when I had morning classes; some were 11 p.m. to 7 a.m., so I could come home and take a nap before going to my afternoon classes. I also used to work weekends.

It wasn't easy to work these jobs and also go to school. I remember one day I woke up and ran for the bus stop without time to check the weather report. I had classes until 1:30, and then I jumped on the bus again and went straight from school to my job at the sweater factory, where I would work from 3:00 until 11:00. I didn't realize that a snowstorm was coming. I had to walk home from work; I didn't have a car, and the buses didn't run that late. The snow was up to my knees. It was terribly cold, and difficult for me to walk in the snow. At one point I fell, and sat in the snow crying before I could make myself get up and go on. I thought I had finally reached the end of my rope, but I kept the thought of my children uppermost in my mind, and somehow found the strength to go on.

It wasn't only my children who helped me to keep pushing forward, though. My identity was not tied up in the low-level jobs I was doing. I never worried about how people would see me, or what they would think. I knew that those jobs were only temporary; they were a means to a greater end. I had the drive and motivation to reach for the sky, even when I did not know how to get there. I did know, though, that I had to keep moving. That internal drive, that ambition, is what keeps you motivated to look for the road you are meant to be on. As human beings, we have the ability to choose our quality of life, and this is a strategic advantage that no other species has. It's important to set positive intentions that inspire you every day, so that your past does not have to determine your future.

After I graduated with my MBA, I finally got a job in the corporate world, but it required creativity and persistence. My green card status was still in limbo, but I was working with an immigration lawyer who told me that I was qualified to apply for a job that would be considered an internship. I applied with an investment firm as a shareholder accountant, and was rejected because I was overqualified! This was ironic, since I had worked so hard for my advanced degree in order to get as good a job as possible. A friend of mine who worked at the same company encouraged me to apply again, and to leave my MBA off my résumé. I did that, and was accepted. I could have applied for higher-level jobs with my qualifications, but I had to keep a low profile and work at the "internship" level due to the issues with my work status. I knew that my MBA would make me better at my job, so I didn't regret having done the extra work to get it, and I felt that it would pay off later, once my visa was settled. My greatest fears still revolved around my immigration status. My lawyer had told my company that my green card was being processed, and I ended up working for that company for twenty-five years.

However, it was imperative that my immigration issues be resolved. My lawyer told me that my visa was a diplomatic visa, and required a waiver from the Nigerian government in order to change my status, to prove that my family, rather than the government, had sponsored my stay in the US. This was exactly what I had been trying to avoid all along…the bribes and politics involved in dealing with the Nigerian government. So, I had to try to solve the situation another way.

Luckily, I did have another option. At a Nigerian party, I had met Paul, who was an American citizen. He had been living in the US for more than twenty years when we met. We danced a couple of times, and exchanged phone numbers. There was a definite attraction between us, and we fell in love. I had learned a lot since my disastrous marriage; my relationship with Paul was very different. When we met, he was working at a Walgreen's in Boston as a pharmacist, but then he found a job at Humana Hospital and moved to Miami, Florida. We took turns visiting each other after he moved out of state. He very much wanted me to move to Miami so we could be close to each other, but I did not want to lose my job; I knew that with my visa issue, I might not be able to get another job…and I might not even be able to stay in the country. The obvious solution was for us to get married; he proposed to me, but getting married wasn't simple.

We didn't want to get married until both of our families were in agreement, as was the custom in Nigeria. We were torn between tradition, and the more modern ways of our generation. The agreement between families was more important in the part of Nigeria where Paul came from, and was a holdover from the days when people believed in human sacrifice. If any member of a family were used as a sacrifice, then the whole family would be outcast. Therefore, according to their custom, it was important that his family communicate with my family to make sure that we were not outcasts. So Paul had to go to Nigeria to talk to my father, and to get his permission for us to marry. My father told him to come back with me, because he wanted me to agree to marry Paul in his presence.

So, once again, I was stuck. I couldn't safely go back to Nigeria until I got married to change my visa status…and I couldn't get married until I went back to Nigeria! I went back to the lawyer again, and went over my options. The waiver I needed for my visa, he said, could be obtained from the Nigerian Embassy in Washington DC, if I could prove that the Nigerian government did not sponsor my exchange mission. I provided all the evidence needed to prove that my family paid for everything—the exchange program, my university education, etc. I took those documents myself to the Nigerian Embassy. The ambassador himself came out and told me that I had to return home; it shouldn't be a problem, he said. His own children, he said, had to return to Nigeria. That was different, though…they could easily come back to the US, because of who they were. Once I went home, it was likely that I would never return to the US. I had done everything I could to prove that the Nigerian government had not sponsored me, but the ambassador had refused to give me the waiver I needed, and there was nothing I could do about it.

When Paul visited me from Florida, I told him about what had happened. I was very downcast and feeling as if my problems would never be resolved. To my amazement, Paul changed the ambassador's mind with a single phone call. It happened that his uncle had gone to school with the ambassador, and was a very close friend of his. He called his uncle, who lived in the United Kingdom, and explained that I needed a waiver that only the ambassador could approve. Paul's uncle called the ambassador and the next thing I knew, Paul traveled to DC with my documents and submitted them. The documents then went in the diplomatic bag to the United States Information Agency for processing. Deep down inside, I had felt there had to be a way to solve this problem. It took a lot of patience, faith, perseverance, and determination to get there, but we made it.

Of course, I know it was fortunate that Paul had this connection. But if he hadn't, I would have gone back to Nigeria, and found a way to come back to the States. Maybe Paul and I would have been married in Nigeria—he had been talking about going back for a while—and then he and I would have found a way around the bribery situation that my family was opposed to. Maybe some other option would have presented itself. But I do know that I wouldn't have given up on my dream. As it turned out, my visa situation was resolved without my marrying Paul, and eventually he and I parted ways.

The power to change our lives lies within each of us, as does the power to realize our dreams, create alternatives, and help to transform the world. We must learn to use our brain for thinking and creating resources by eradicating the negative things that hinder us from moving forward. We must direct our lives toward positive energy. We should not allow our lives to be shaped by what people think of us. Our past should not determine our potential. Each of us must create and nurture a self-image, an idea of who we can be and who we are, that is separate from our immediate circumstances.

I know what a challenge this can be, because I have done it myself. And because I have changed my life by creating my own agenda and strategy, I believe that ever reader of this book should make sure they are in control of their own agenda, too. That is the only way you can live a satisfactory life. I want to help people avoid one of the mistakes I made…or at least, if you make the same mistake, I want to show you how to break out of it, as I did.

Often, we surrender our power to others and play the victim, forgetting that who we have become, and who we will be, is in our control. I stand accused of having done that for twenty-five years in corporate America. I played the victim until things had gone too far, and my frustration was clouding any chance I had for progress. I was following someone else's agenda, rather than my own, working hard and expecting to be appreciated, waiting for a raise and a bonus at the end of the year, and hoping that my job would still be there for me as long as I was a good worker. After reading this book, I hope that anyone who thinks they can follow their dreams by allowing someone else to control their agenda will wake up, and realize that the only person who can set a path to your dreams is you!

Let me share with you what happened to shake me out of my complacency, and how I developed my personal vision and business.

CHAPTER VII

How I Found My Life Purpose

MY WAKE-UP CALL CAME on an August morning at 11:31 a.m., when I received an e-mail from the president of my company with a link to an important video message. The message was an announcement that the company would be moving some employees and jobs out of state. A meeting was scheduled in which the moves to five different states would be explained. Every employee whose job moved was expected to move with the job…and my job was in that category.

I had some serious thinking to do. I had been working at this company for twenty-five years. I started as a shareholder accountant, and was now working in bank reconciliation, which was a better job than the one I had started with, but still in no way reflective of my education or abilities. I had been thinking for a long time about quitting. But I was afraid of not being able to pay my bills and put food on the table if I quit, so I had been waiting for another opportunity to present itself. I kept looking for a different job in the same company, believing that there wasn't a better company in that field. In retrospect, I realize that I was so afraid of taking any risk or venturing out on my own that I didn't really research other companies in my field. I lacked confidence, and had become complacent where I was. My company had even started promoting people I had trained into positions above me, which was ridiculous. When I asked my supervisor about this, she simply shrugged and said that people who didn't like their situation had left. I attended a networking event at which the speaker said that if you are being passed over for promotion, and your boss doesn't like you, then you should move on, because nothing is going to change. I felt as if she were speaking directly to me; and at the same time, it was reassuring to know that I was not the only person in the corporate world who was having these types of frustrations. Even with all this, though, it had seemed impossible for me to quit this job unless I had something else waiting for me, due to my challenging family circumstances.

After I broke up with Paul, I met Jake. He had been with the media at a Nigerian meeting that he was moderating. He noticed me when I got up and asked a question, and after the meeting, he approached me and wanted to get to know me better. We became good friends, and we dated for seven years before we got married. Shortly after we were married, he was diagnosed with throat cancer. After that was treated, he got lung cancer, and then a brain tumor, and finally ataxia, which caused him to have seizures and fall, after which he would be unable to get up by himself. This was a lot for both of us to handle. I was grateful for my Christian faith; at times, that was all that kept me going.

When this mandatory job transfer came up, I had to weigh the pros and cons. It was frightening to think of losing my income, but on the other hand, if I moved out of state, I would be paying double taxes, in the state where I lived and in the state where I worked. My company would not reimburse me for mileage because the distance between my current home and the out-of-state jobsite was less than fifty miles. But round trip, that would be almost a hundred miles a day, and I couldn't afford gas plus wear and tear on my car…not on the salary I was currently making. Additionally, I couldn't afford all that time spent driving, and it wasn't safe for Jake to have me that far from home. He needed me nearby to take him to doctor's appointments, and it wasn't safe to leave him for long periods of time. I had gotten to a point where I couldn't afford to wait any longer for an opportunity; I had to make my own.

Luckily for me, although my job was stagnant and frustrating, I hadn't allowed it to stop me from pursuing personal growth, and eventually my commitment to exploring my passions and talents would be what allowed me to take my life in a satisfying direction. I cannot stress enough how important it is to make time for the things that call to you on a deep and compelling level. Even if it's not clear to you how your life will change or how your goals will reach fruition, keep exploring who you are called to be in the world. If you are attuned to the best truths about yourself, you are far more likely to recognize an opportunity when it comes.

When I realized how bored and frustrated I was at my job, I started looking for a new challenge. I looked into what I could to for the community relations department of the company I worked for, and I started volunteer work. It made me feel good, even though in the back of my mind I wished there would be an official job opening in that department so I could transfer. But the volunteer work required me to put a variety of skills and interests to good use. I worked on middle school transformation days, where we would paint, do landscaping clean-up, rearrange the school library, etc. I volunteered at the TV station WGBH for a high school quiz; I tutored underserved middle school students on interviewing skills; I coached students about how to find career paths that matched their skills; and I did remedial reading work with students on Saturdays.

For a long time, I had known that counseling, coaching, and training were my calling. Friends and family members considered me a resource for talking through and finding solutions to problems, and every time I used my innate talents in this way, I would be told that I was in the wrong business…that I should open a counseling business. Although I heard this, I didn't take it literally—at least, not yet. However, I continued to hone and develop my talents in this area.

When I volunteered with students, I learned how to carefully attune my coaching to meet them where they were in their lives, while making sure that they understood the skills and resources they had to take them forward into the future. In working with church organizations, I learned a lot about group dynamics and teamwork, and how to facilitate communication and cooperation among various personalities. As time went by, I realized more and more that using my talents to help people achieve their goals and be fulfilled was what made me happy. In retrospect, I now clearly understand that volunteering and joining civic organizations, such as women's business associations or other peer-based groups, is essential for networking. The idea of networking is often overwhelming to people; very few of us enjoy going out and "selling" who we are. This is why it is essential to understand the value of volunteering and civic/community service. Being yourself, showing your talents to the people around you—that is the best networking you will ever do. When people know who you are, opportunities start to open up around you. Churches are especially powerful places to let your light shine, because you are usually surrounded by people with a wide variety of professions and enthusiasms. Giving your best to your church family is one of the most effective forms of service.

I had arrived at a crossroads of my life: my job was no longer sustainable, and the move they wanted me to make was impossible, given the circumstances with my husband. The time had come for me to use my talents in a more focused way to create a new life for myself. I came home from work one day, and in the mail I found a post card telling me that someone had given me a gift…a book called *The Millionaire Maker*. I laughed, but I did read the post card, and I set it aside rather than throwing it away. It took me two more days to call the 1-800 number on the card. I was told that the book would be on its way if I paid $6.00 for shipping and handling, so I did.

When I received and read the book, I was impressed with the wealth-building strategies they outlined, so I called the company and signed up for their mentoring program. Prior to this, I had applied for a mentoring program at my job, but had not been accepted. The mentoring program associated with *The Millionaire Maker* started with an assessment of strengths and skills. The assessment confirmed that one of my strongest skills is consultation (or counseling, or coaching). This wasn't a surprise to me, but this was the first time I'd had it absolutely affirmed in connection with the idea of making money or changing careers…it was quite different to have a professional test tell me that I should have a career as a counselor, as opposed to being told that by friends and family.

Right away, the mentoring I received through the program began to change my outlook. I had always believed I didn't have what it took to be independent…I was continually asking myself, "What if I fail?" But as Michelangelo said, "The greatest danger for most of us is not that we aim too high and miss it, but that we aim too low and reach it." Through the work I did with my mentor, I registered my e-commerce company, which I called Unlimited Delight, LLC. I chose this name because I planned to own multiple businesses that would produce multiple streams of income. My plans came to fruition: now I own a coaching business and an online store, and my next goal is to start real estate investments. I became super-charged, and so confident that I am ready to grab any business opportunities that present themselves.

At the recommendation of my mentor, I hired a coach. The experience of being coached just reaffirmed even more strongly for me that this is what I wanted to do in my own career. Being coached showed me how to be a better coach, and taught me a lot about interacting with clients. My coach was very professional; when we met, he clearly stated his rules, and also sent them to me in writing. He let me know that if a scheduled session was cancelled without enough notice, it would be forfeited without a refund. He told me that I would be given an assignment at the end of every session, and that the assignment should be completed and faxed to him a day before the next session, so he would have time to review it and be ready to discuss it during the session. Our sessions were set for 30 minutes per week, for 12 weeks.

This wasn't the only coach I had—I deeply appreciated the value of coaching, and I have had several coaches for different areas of my business, including investments, internet marketing, and e-commerce. One of the most valuable lessons I learned from my mentor is that it's a waste of time to try to reinvent the wheel. Whatever you want to do, chances are someone else has already done it, and if you can follow in their footsteps or improve on a system that's in place, you'll be using your time much more effectively than if you start from scratch. That's one of the most important things that coaching does: it maximizes your available time by giving you access to proven expertise that you can internalize and build on.

My first coach and I focused on my career change—but that's not the term we used. We called it my life purpose, and for the first time, I truly realized that what I do to make a living can and should align with my calling in the world. My coach started giving me assignments that would help me to state clearly what I was trying to achieve in life, and how I planned to achieve it. Once he knew what my life purpose was, he was able to help me more effectively. He assisted me in identifying the steps I needed to take in order to live my purpose. My coach taught me to make my life purpose statement a firmly ingrained part of daily living. I would find a quiet, comfortable spot to meditate and reflect on my purpose, and I would envision what my life would be like in the future once I was living my purpose. This vision exercise included all areas of my life: financial, career/business, free time, family time, health/appearance, personal relationships, and community relationships. I wrote down my visions and shared them with my coach.

This exercise was invaluable in helping me to find out what stood out the most for me, and what my biggest insights were. Setting goals with affirmation helped me to move forward and achieve my goals. The meditation taught to me by my coach was necessary to help me focus on my vision and on the path from where I am now, to where I need to be. My coach asked me to set 101 goals, and prioritize them. Then he made me decide what my breakthrough goal would be. Would it be landing a promotion, meeting a sales goal, changing jobs, expanding my business…? I had realized that my life purpose is to tell my story, in order to empower and inspire others to reach their highest potentials and fulfill their life purpose, and perhaps tell their own stories, one person at a time. Together, we will transform the world and make it a better place to be. And so, I decided that my breakthrough goal would be the publication of this book, and I set a date of July 8, 2013. I am confident that this book will give me the exposure and platform I need to fulfill my purpose of inspiring and empowering others.

When I think about my life purpose, I could have gone in a couple of different directions to reach more people with coaching. I could have chosen to expand my online store, because I have always wanted to own a store, and I enjoy that work. But the book has the potential to reach more people, faster, who need help in defining and meeting their goals. Publication of my book won't mean that my other goals disappear—the book is just the first goal. My coach and I have mapped out marketing strategies that I will follow step by step, and then there is the rest of my goal list to start on. One of the greatest benefits of having a coach is the help given with prioritizing goals. When you're in the middle of your own vision and ambition, it's easy to lose sight of where you're going, and why. Your coach helps you to stay focused.

Now that you have heard my story, and you know how I got to the point of being ready to put my life purpose in motion, I'd like to share with you my thoughts, observations, and philosophy about how all of us can take charge of our lives, and live in a more abundant and fulfilling way. I know I am fortunate to have the inner strength and fortitude to stick to my guns and stand my ground. Once I had made the decision to leave my job and change my life, I started to feel emotionally strong, and was able to keep my priorities straight. I now know it's time to help as many people as possible, and motivate them to achieve their dreams. It's time to help people realize that each individual is unique, with God-given talents. If we remain focused and avoid distractions, we will self-actualize and amplify our gifts. I hope that my message will bring awareness to the reader about the importance of making changes in our lives.

It's essential to be realistic about the fact that change involves risk—and for many of us, risk is a scary concept.

However, there is a difference between positive risk and negative risk. When we follow our dreams and act with our intuition on high alert, we are far more likely to recognize an opportunity (which is a positive risk) and take advantage of it. We need to have the courage to get out of our comfort zones and try something new and different, even though that could be both terrifying and thrilling. We must have confidence that the positive risks we take will have a worthwhile outcome. You are not alone in your struggle to find your path, and it's good to learn to recognize when and how to seek help when you need it. The kind and wise support of others can create the safety we need to take chances that will lead to happiness and fulfillment. In the end, those benefits far outweigh the risks we had to take. But, as with everything, the ability to take chances is a learning process that requires understanding and practice.

We may not understand what it means to take chances if we do not get the help we need to go from where we are to where we want to be. I had already started writing this book when I was introduced to one of my coaches, Jack Canfield, and his book *The Success Principles*. In this book, Jack teaches us how important it is for every individual living on this earth to take 100% responsibility for their lives. I believe him when he says that "the real truth—and the one lesson this whole book is based on—is that there is only one person responsible for the quality of the life you live. That person is you." It is quite easy for us to blame our environment, the economy, the president, our parents, our friends, our siblings, etc. for everything that is going wrong in our lives, without ever remembering that the outcome of the events in our lives is directly related to the decisions we make—and those are our responsibility. The only way we can liberate ourselves is to take the first step, by accepting responsibility for our decisions.

It took me a long time to realize that I have created my current conditions, and that I can create them and re-create them at will, by taking 100% responsibility for my life. The idea of taking responsibility can be frightening. It's important to realize as well that it's okay to ask for help. Of course, it is possible that people will say no, but that shouldn't prevent you from asking. It's another facet of learning about positive risks. If you choose to feel rejected or think that everybody hates you, that won't solve any problems. Rather, such feelings compound your problems and cloud your chances of seeing the possibilities in front of you.

I remember the mistakes I made myself, before I learned these principles. When things did not turn out as planned, I did not ask myself the appropriate question, which would have been, "How did I create this situation for myself?" I remembered to say to myself that maybe I wasn't working hard enough, and then I would strive to fix the situation by working harder. The signals were there, but I didn't pay attention to them. I remember one of the supervisors at my job saying to me one day, "You work too hard—that's not the way to do it." Perhaps he was trying to help me; I should have asked him what he meant. But I didn't follow up with him to ask what he meant. If I had taken that next positive risk to ask for more information, I would have had a different result. We need to make sure that our minds are open and clear, so that new opportunities and possibilities have a chance to show up.

When I talk about taking 100% responsibility for your life, it's with the understanding that things happen to people that are outside of their direct control. Taking responsibility means making life-affirming decisions about the circumstances you are in. People experience traumas of all kinds—physical, emotional, and psychological. It may be challenging to learn how to carry the weight of those traumas gracefully, but it is possible to do, and more importantly, your example may inspire and heal someone else who is suffering. Part of the idea of asking for help includes seeking counseling and healing when you need them. And asking for help is a key part of taking responsibility. Sometimes that is one of the most confusing concepts for people…asking for help seems weak, or they think they should be able to do everything on their own. But knowing when you need someone else's support, information, or wisdom is a sign of strength. Taking responsibility includes seeking and accepting the good and healing things that other people can give you. And it also includes giving support and strength to others.

One of the most meaningful incidents in my own journey was my realization that I needed to listen to the supportive information that people who cared about me were providing to me. I got stuck in my routine dead-end job because I lacked confidence, and anyone meeting me could read that about me easily. When you don't have confidence in yourself, other people lose confidence in you as well, even if you are competent and well-qualified. One day a co-worker said to me, "Regina, you know more than you give yourself credit for." I recognized this as a compliment, and I thought about it for several days. I said to myself, *She is telling you that you can trust yourself.* I realized that I had a lot to give and to contribute, but I wasn't letting it out because I was afraid of being wrong. My fear of failure was holding me back in a very painful and self-limiting way.

When I complained about not being promoted at work, my boss said to me, "People leave if they don't like it." Although this was a very strange and inappropriate thing for her to say, it made me think, and fueled my determination to do something about my situation. The choice was mine, to be offended by what she'd said, or to put it to good use.

I want to emphasize that getting the courage to leave, and finding what I wanted to do next, took determination. It wasn't easy. I felt as if I were just stuck on the treadmill at my job, with no time or energy left over to figure out what my next move might be. Many people I know were also in dead-end jobs that they don't enjoy, and I found myself wondering whether those feelings of frustration and lack of fulfillment were just normal. I felt stuck and discouraged. I had lost my vision of where I wanted to go with my life.

CREDIT TO MY COACH
CHRISTIAN MICKELSEN

CHAPTER VIII

What You Can Do to Take Responsibility for Your Life

LIKE MANY PEOPLE, I had never been taught that there are a few simple yet very powerful steps we can take to find and secure an ideal career. I want to share these steps with you. I am the right person to share this information because I had to learn it myself and act on it. If you feel stuck and unhappy in your work, please take hope from my example. I worked in jobs I didn't enjoy, for twenty-six years. I know what it's like to feel stuck and confused. And I also know, because I have done it myself, that it is possible to rise out of your dead-end job and find your life purpose. It is extremely important to have a mentor or coach who helps you to discover your talents, and who holds you accountable for putting them to work toward your dream.

Step #1: CLARIFY YOUR DIRECTION

It is challenging to find your ideal job unless you're clear about what that really means to you. Many times, people buy into what they think they "should" be doing, rather than following their true passion. Once you begin to understand your life purpose, you can create a vision that clarifies what you need in order to become motivated and inspired to pursue the ideal career you are working toward.

When I started thinking about my dream job, it was scary at first, to think about how high I was reaching. Because I have an online store, coaching business, real estate investing business, and am always looking for additional opportunities, my ideal income would be a million dollars per year or more. It's okay to dream big—the bigger the dream, the more you are challenged, and the higher the rewards.

My mentors and coaches cheered me on, telling me that I could do it. When I started thinking about my dream job, I knew I wanted a job where I would be able to take control of my schedule, and set my own agenda. I wanted free time to travel and spend with my family, and to structure my business so that it would generate profit both when I was there, and when I was away…a self-sustaining income stream. I wanted to spend most of my time with people who inspire me and who have insights to share, such as authors Jack Canfield (who is also one of my coaches), Jim Stovall, Natalie Ledwell (a law of attraction evangelist), Dan Janal (president and founder of PR Leads Plus), and the well-known inspirational writer Deepak Chopra. I am living this dream, and recently contributed to a book they co-authored, called *Ready, Aim, Captivate*, which brought together experts, entrepreneurs, and authorities on how to take your individual message and use it to reach out to others, change lives, and captivate hearts. I was proud to be included in this book, which focuses on ordinary people who have overcome challenges to follow their dreams.

When you start thinking about clarifying your direction, keep in mind that not only is it okay to dream big, it's essential! Don't be self-conscious or embarrassed by your dreams. If you have a passion for something, if you can envision it, that means the seed of it is deep within you, just waiting to blossom. Embrace your dreams in all their scope and complexity, and surround yourself with people who believe in your dreams and in you.

Step #2: STRATEGIZE YOUR ACTIONS

Once you have a picture of what your dream job looks like, you need a step-by-step plan to get you there easily. Prioritizing your steps and setting up a solid plan makes the process realistic, manageable, and enjoyable. Sketch a plan that will help you get to your goal, and follow that plan, starting with the first step. Resources that can help you might include reading a book about careers, visiting a career counselor, taking a personality test to identify your talents and strengths, or taking a skills inventory test to gain additional insight into what you do well and what you love to do. You can list all your strengths and passions, and brainstorm practical ways to put them to work. You can consider ideas from trusted friends, colleagues, and mentors who might have ideas that you haven't even considered.

When I realized that my life purpose was to share my story with the world in order to change lives and captivate hearts, I knew that my first step needed to be to write this book, promote it, and market it to the world. I am strategizing around how and where to promote my book to get it in front of my target market, which includes teenage mothers, businessmen and women, women in the corporate world, people struggling with depression, and people who have struggled to survive. I have researched and followed opportunities to start making my voice heard. I have done two radio interviews, and contributed a chapter to two different books written by well-known authors: *Ready, Aim, Captivate* and *Wounded, Survive, Thrive*.

I know that my plan of action is solid and that I am moving in the right direction, because I am already seeing results. Thanks to one of the radio interviews I did, a magazine that caters to baby boomers wants to advertise my book to its readers. I will be pursuing more radio and TV interviews, as well as press releases, readings, and other appearances to publicize the book. The key to the book's success is to have a platform and publicity in place even before the book is published—and because I have done that, there was buzz about and interest in this book before it was written. You now hold in your hands the result of effective strategic planning.

Sometimes when people think about planning and strategy, it sounds like a tedious chore—and it can be, when you're planning for someone else's success, or working on someone else's project. If you've been stuck in a dead-end job for a long time, the idea of planning and goal-setting can seem overwhelming. Just remember that it's different when you are pursuing your life purpose, and when you are seeing immediate and powerful results. Another way to think about planning is to see it as a road map, and the steps along the way as road signs that point you to the next mile marker closer to your destination. Planning and strategy can be exciting and fun—and as you see your goal on the horizon, the next steps become clearer and even more invigorating.

Step #3: UPGRADE YOUR SKILLS

Sometimes the only thing standing between us and our dream job is a skills upgrade. Maybe you've always loved graphic design, but you need to take a course in web programming in order to put that to work as a web designer. Or maybe you have all the technical skills you need, but you could use some work on your interview skills. Maybe you need to learn about or brush up on business skills so you can start your own company. The good news is that it's never too late to learn! Sometimes, especially if you've had a lot of struggles in your early life, the idea of going to school can seem daunting or depressing. This is one of the areas of life in which it can be very important not to decide what you can do based on your past. Learning something you want to learn, as an adult in charge of your own education, is a very different experience from high school, or even college. You may be going back to college to earn a different degree or take classes, but your motivation will be different, and your skill set as a learner will be more mature and more focused. And don't forget that online or distance learning makes things much more flexible for you.

In my own journey, I started with webinars and teleclasses. I went to publicity workshops to add skills I did not have before—I knew it was important for me to learn how to publish and promote a book, since this is the cornerstone of my life purpose and goals. I took coaching classes, which I needed in order to understand how the coaching industry works, and how to define my niche and target market. I took internet marketing classes to learn how to maximize the potential of my online store. I attended conferences and enjoyed audio and video broadcasts from industry leaders whom I admire and want to emulate. These were all new skills for me, and it was both enjoyable and necessary to acquire them.

Step #4: OPTIMIZE YOUR ENVIRONMENT

Your environment includes the people you surround yourself with, the atmosphere you're in at work and at home, and all the factors that make up your experience of daily life. There are facets of your environment affecting you on a daily basis that you might not even think about, such as the radio station that plays at your office or in your car. Your environment also includes self-care, such as diet and exercise, as well as your relationships with other people. All of these factors should be as supportive and healthy as possible.

It's especially important to look at the ways in which your personal relationships are interacting with your dreams. If you're committed to finding work that you love, but your friends tell you that's crazy, and you should just take your paycheck and enjoy life on the weekends, that might not be a supportive environment. You don't necessarily need to ditch that group of friends, but you may wish to add time with others who are serious about pursuing their dreams and supporting yours. By doing so, you're already much closer to being set up for success.

Make a list of things you could change about your environment to make it more supportive. Also make a list of the things that you already find to be extremely supportive and inspiring in your daily life. Be honest about the changes you need to make. Some changes may go back to #3, upgrading your skills. If, for example, you find it a challenge to stay organized, and you spend a lot of time spinning your wheels, you may want to take a class in business management or time management. If you don't have the physical energy you want or need, you may benefit from targeted education about nutrition or other self-care. If there are people in your life who are negative and draining, you might want to consider acquiring skills to draw boundaries with those people, and align yourself with like-minded friends and colleagues.

In my case, I made changes that allowed me to optimize my time. As I've mentioned, I am my husband's caregiver, and that commitment means I have to be very smart about how I manage my time. I set boundaries around talking to friends who just wanted to chat, and spent that time instead on classes, webinars, and teleseminars. I hired a virtual assistant who does administrative and clerical work in my online store, so that I can focus on the more important tasks of getting my business to the next level. I cleaned out the clutter in my workspace and created a different organizational system so that I don't have to waste creative time looking for files, or sorting through a messy office. I hired a housekeeper once a week, and I created a schedule for shopping and cooking. Once I completed these changes to my environment, business began to move faster and faster. I now have enough time to respond thoughtfully to important e-mails, and to carefully read business documents that require my attention. I have the time I need with my husband, and I have time for myself, to exercise and rest.

When you are thinking about your environment, don't forget to allow yourself time to restore and relax. Down time is essential to creativity and productivity. Meditation, yoga, a favorite sport, exercise, reading, handicrafts, music, creative arts—these are all things that sustain you psychologically, spiritually, and emotionally. Make sure that your environment supports you as a whole person, as well as supporting your dream job.

Step #5: MASTER YOUR PSYCHOLOGY

This may be the most important step to help you move confidently into work you love. Sometimes, no matter what you do to create change, there is something underneath all your positive actions that still holds you back. Please be reassured that it is completely normal to encounter fears, doubts, and limiting beliefs when you're considering a new career path.

There are many excellent ways to work with these psychological factors so that they no longer have any power over you and your success. The first is simply to become aware of them. Knowledge is power. Once you start to bring these processes out of hiding and into the light of your awareness, you can work with them, and release them. In my coaching programs, I offer my clients a lot of powerful strategies to master their psychology once and for all. It makes a huge difference to have someone support you in the process of releasing fears, doubts, and limiting beliefs that have been holding you back. In fact, hiring a coach was one of the single most important steps I took to help master my own psychology and go for my goals.

I'd like to give you an example of how I coached someone out of a self-limiting belief. Donald was a carpenter who did some work on my house. He didn't have a car, so every time he did any work for me, I would have to pick him up from his house, and drive him to my house. One day I told him that he would have to start paying me for these rides; it wasn't appropriate for me to hire him and then be his car service. His work was good, but he didn't charge very much, with the result that he branded himself poor. He didn't like the idea of having to reimburse me for rides. This started a conversation between us. I told him that I would give him a piece of free advice that other people would pay me good money to get, and that if it worked out for him and he wanted more advice from me, then he would have to pay me (my arrangement with him was that his payment consisted of referring other clients to me for coaching).

I told him to stop calling himself poor, because God had created him rich, and that was why God had blessed him with the talent to make things. It would be up to Donald to use those talents to create wealth for himself. If he chose to underutilize those God-given talents and brand himself poor, then he would remain poor. The difference between the rich and the poor is the way they think about and do things. God never meant for anybody to be poor; we all have talents. Some of us recognize that talent when we are young, such as people who go on to be professional actors, singers, etc. Those people have mentors and coaches. But it's even more important, I told Donald, for ordinary people like us, who may not recognize our talents, to have help in figuring out what God has given us. I told him that he was in complete control of his life, and that if he didn't like it, he could turn it around.

I asked Donald what he could do other than finish carpentry. He told me that he made picture frames and furniture, such as foldable side tables. I asked him to bring me a sample of his work, and he did. I told him I would like to keep the samples at my house for a month, to show to my friends who might place some orders. Fifteen of my friends and I placed orders worth $1500. Donald had told me that he didn't have anything to do between jobs. I told him that people would rather work with someone who had transportation, and that at the beginning of a job, he should take a deposit and use it to rent a car for the duration of the contract. I also told him that he should take his beautiful fine woodworking to neighborhood stores and place them on consignment.

He took my advice, and soon sold $20,000 worth of items. His building carpentry work also picked up, because I helped him to design a flyer to put in community centers and neighborhood stores. He began to get regular calls for work, and he no longer needed a ride from anybody. He came back to me and paid me $2500, and ever since then he has been my client, coming back for more and more advice. I told him to employ his wife and neighborhood children for the parts of his work that didn't require his exact finesse and attention to detail, and now business is booming for him, as well as benefiting his wife and the children he employs. He will never call himself poor again, and he has referred five clients to me.

Donald didn't have to change his way of thinking very much in order for his life to open up in a spectacular way. The change he made was well within his reach, but it was deeply significant. However, it took an outside observer to help him identify and remove his psychological roadblock. Donald is only one of many people whom I have helped into abundance and a fulfilling life.

CHAPTER IX

My Hope for Every Reader's Future

YOU MUST PAY ATTENTION to the five steps I have outlined in the previous chapter. These are things you might need a coach to help you with, if you want to go from where you are now to where you want to be. You have to live your purpose in life. As we go through life, we have a choice concerning our talents, and it's an important choice. We can choose to struggle through life, attempting to thrive in activities that really don't align with our talents, or we can identify and celebrate our talents. There is a prevailing philosophy that success and strength can be found in overcoming weaknesses. But that is often a frustrating and self-defeating way to live. You have only so much time and energy in this life…would you rather use those things to honor your strengths, or to defeat your weaknesses?

Of course, to use our talents, we must know what they are. Do you know what your talents are? Do you even know how to recognize them operating in your daily life? If the answer to those questions is "no," then now is the time to follow the advice in this book to discover what your life purpose is. I did not know mine until I found a mentor and a coach to help me observe myself and to hold me accountable, making sure that my actions are progressing toward my goals.

I want you to live your life purpose. My purpose is to tell my life story in this book, and distribute it to as many people as possible so that those who read it can resonate with what I am saying here, and use some or all of this information to change their lives for the better. I want you to know that if what you are doing now is not yielding the desired outcome, you have the ability to change it to produce a favorable outcome. You and only you can do this for yourself. You have read my story now, and you know that I understand these principles from my own life. I spent a long time coming up with complaints and excuses to justify being stuck, but things just continued to get worse until I make the decision to change my life.

Change has to come from within you. Change always comes with some level of risk, but you must be willing to take the risk and persevere to create the life of your dreams. The steps I have outlined for you may lead you to a career change, or to improve your working conditions…or you may find a different way of thinking, or of organizing your life at home. Whatever change you are called to make that aligns with your deepest truth, that will be a positive change, and will yield results that you can't yet anticipate or fully understand.

My goal in this book is to inspire and empower people to be who they were born to be. Human beings were born to be creative, but somewhere along the line, most of us lose sight of that. Think back to when you were a child, and somebody asked you what you wanted to be when you grew up. What was your first answer? Your creativity lies in that answer, but chances are, you never consciously activated it. You need to have the burning desire to choose the direction of your life, and rekindle that fire you had growing up. Engage yourself now. When you believe in the engagement of now, it doesn't matter where your life has been in the past. One of the most productive human desires is the desire for control. You have the ability to take control of your life, now and in the future. You need to take charge, because a charged and inspired life generates a different level of energy, which keeps you pushed and challenged to achieve. You find yourself fully engaged, and more satisfied.

If you are feeling that there is more to life than you are living now—there is. If you are feeling that you could do better—of course you can! If you are feeling that you could work less and make more money—you're right! Life is all about choices. The choices we make in life are behind our successes and failures. Believe in yourself, be confident that you are good at what you do. Your focus should be on the bigger picture, and on greatness, rather than on the trivial and petty distractions of daily life. Don't be afraid to try new things; greatness lies across unexplored territory. It is easy to step into greatness when you consciously activate your drive for control, for competence, for caring, for connection, and for identity.

When you think about the process of change, try to change your vocabulary…it's automatic to equate change with pain, but turn it around and focus on gain! Try to think about the potential, rather than about fear. How can you bring joy and adventure to the process you're fearful about? Focus on the potential positives, and envision what you want your life to be like.

We are always at the crossroads of opportunity and change. Many of us come across these opportunities every day, and never see them. My situation became so intolerable that I was forced to look around me and see the opportunities that were always there. I am finding that those doors are wide open for me, and for everyone. You just have to be looking in the right place. Each day is a gift that you should feel a deep desire to use to the utmost. When you take the leap of faith in yourself, you are taking charge of your agenda, and of your life purpose. Your place in the world is not to follow someone else's agenda: it is to find and make your own, and surround yourself with people who support you in where you are going.

In closing, I want to thank you for the opportunity to share my story with you. I am confident that in learning how I came to take charge of my destiny and find my life purpose, you will be inspired to do the same. I wish you courage, joy, vision, and unlimited delight in your journey. For more information, you may email me at reginaozoemela@yahoo.com and I will personally respond to your email within 24 to 48 hours.